Know Your Numbers

Bunches of Buttons

Counting by Tens

Special thanks to our advisers for their expertise:

Stuart Farm, M.Ed., Mathematics Lecturer
University of North Dakota, Grand Forks

Susan Kesselring, M.A., Literacy Educator
Rosemount–Apple Valley–Eagan (Minnesota) School District

by Michael Dahl
illustrated by Zachary Trover

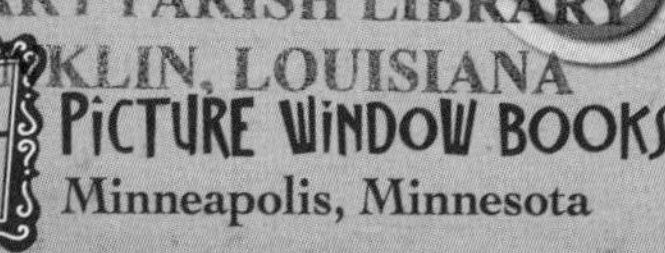

PICTURE WINDOW BOOKS
Minneapolis, Minnesota

Editor: Christianne Jones
Designer: Jaime Martens
Page Production: Angela Kilmer
Creative Director: Keith Griffin
Editorial Director: Carol Jones
The illustrations in this book were created digitally.

Picture Window Books
5115 Excelsior Boulevard
Suite 232
Minneapolis, MN 55416
877-845-8392
www.picturewindowbooks.com

Printed in the United States of America.

Library of Congress Cataloging-in-Publication Data
Dahl, Michael.
Bunches of buttons : counting by tens / by Michael Dahl ; illustrated by Zachary Trover.
p. cm. — (Know your numbers)
Includes bibliographical references and index.
ISBN 1-4048-1315-2 (hardcover)
1. Counting—Juvenile literature. 2. Addition—Juvenile literature. 3. Buttons—Juvenile literature. I. Trover, Zachary, ill. II. Title.

QA113.D325 2006
513.2'11—dc22 2005021817

I'm Billy Ben.
I'm 10 years old,
and I like buttons.

I collect bunches and bunches of buttons.
I put them in an empty jelly jar.

I put TEN red buttons in my jelly jar.
I'll keep looking. Maybe I'll find more!

10

I find ten orange buttons in my brother's smelly sneaker.

TWENTY buttons
in my jelly jar.

I find ten purple buttons in a pink, plastic pig.

THIRTY buttons
in my jelly jar.

I find ten green buttons in my sister's sock drawer.

FORTY buttons
in my jelly jar.

I find ten pink buttons in my mom's potted plant.

FIFTY buttons
in my jelly jar.

I find ten blue buttons in my lockable lunch box.

SIXTY buttons
in my jelly jar.
60

I find ten yellow buttons under the sink.

10 20 30 40 50 60 70

SEVENTY buttons
in my jelly jar.

I find ten white buttons in a purple pillowcase.

10	20	30	40	50	60	70	80

80

EIGHTY buttons
in my jelly jar.

I find ten brown buttons in a chest.

NINETY buttons
in my jelly jar.

I find ten black buttons in a brass buckled box.

ONE HUNDRED buttons in my jelly jar.

Now my jar is full. I can't wait for show-and-tell!

Fun Facts

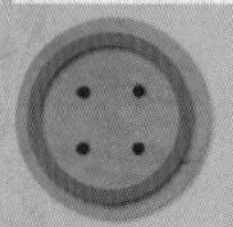

Buttons can be made of metal, wood, plastic, jewels, glass, and even seashells.

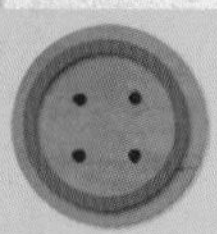

The word *button* comes from a French word that means "flower bud."

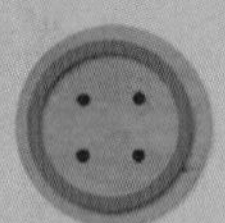

Hundreds of years ago, King Francis I of France ordered a special jacket decorated with more than 13,000 gold buttons.

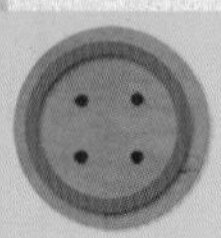

Police and fire fighters wear uniforms with the names of their cities stamped on the buttons.

On the Web

FactHound offers a safe, fun way to find Internet sites related to this book. All of the sites on FactHound have been researched by our staff.

1. Visit *www.facthound.com*
2. Type in this special code for age-appropriate sites: 1404813152
3. Click on the FETCH IT button.

Your trusty FactHound will fetch the best sites for you!

Find the Numbers

Now you have finished reading the story, but a surprise still awaits you. Hidden in each picture is a multiple of ten from 10 to 100. Can you find them all?

10–in the bush
20–on the shoe
30–on the pig's nose
40–on the lamp
50–in the plant
60–on the boy's ear
70–on the spray bottle
80–on the bedpost
90–on the opening of the chest
100–on the buckle

Look for all of the books in the Know Your Numbers series:

Ants At the Picnic: Counting by Tens
1-4048-1318-7

Bunches of Buttons: Counting by Tens
1-4048-1315-2

Downhill Fun: A Counting Book About Winter
1-4048-0579-6

Eggs and Legs: Counting By Twos
1-4048-0945-7

Footprints in the Snow: Counting By Twos
1-4048-0946-5

From the Garden: A Counting Book About Growing Food
1-4048-0578-8

Hands Down: Counting By Fives
1-4048-0948-1

Lots of Ladybugs! Counting By Fives
1-4048-0944-9

On the Launch Pad: A Counting Book About Rockets
1-4048-0581-8

One Big Building: A Counting Book About Construction
1-4048-0580-X

One Checkered Flag: A Counting Book About Racing
1-4048-0576-1

One Giant Splash: A Counting Book About the Ocean
1-4048-0577-X

Pie for Piglets: Counting By Twos
1-4048-0943-0

Plenty of Petals: Counting by Tens
1-4048-1317-9

Speed, Speed Centipede! Counting by Tens
1-4048-1316-0

Starry Arms: Counting By Fives
1-4048-0947-3

Tail Feather Fun: Counting By Tens
1-4048-1319-5

Toasty Toes: Counting By Tens
1-4048-1320-9